Y0-BBW-413

H is for
Hong Kong

A Primer in Pictures

香港

By Tricia Morrissey • Illustrations by Elizabeth Briel

To my parents, both dedicated travelers. Thanks to Albert, who dreamed up this project, and to Roy, the best possible companion for Hong Kong — and everywhere else. — E.B.

For Mark, who built me a beautiful kitchen while I imagined a distant city. — T.M.

H is for Hong Kong — A Primer in Pictures
By Tricia Morrissey
Illustrations by Elizabeth Briel

Copyright ©2008 ThingsAsian Press

All rights reserved under international copyright conventions. No part of the contents of this book may be reproduced or utilized in any form or by any means, electronic or mechanical, including photocopying and recording, or by any information storage and retrieval system, without the written consent of the publisher.

Chinese translation by Michelle Lai Wong
Cover and book design by Janet McKelpin
Book production by Paul Tomanpos, Jr.

For information regarding permissions, write to:
ThingsAsian Press
3230 Scott Street
San Francisco, California 94123 USA
info@thingsasianpress.com
www.thingsasianpress.com
Printed in Singapore by Tien Wah Press

ISBN 10: 1-934159-13-1
ISBN 13: 978-1-934159-13-2

"An inch of gold cannot buy an inch of time."

cùn   jīn   nán   mǎi   cùn   guāng   yīn
寸　金　難　買　寸　光　陰

– Chinese Proverb

Imagine visiting a new city today. Imagine flying to Hong Kong! Journey through this wonderful, busy place and what will you see? Soaring skyscrapers? Shiny, amber goldfish? Ferry boats sailing on a sparkling bay? Turn the page and imagine, because today H is for Hong Kong.

想像去一個新城市
遊覽，想像飛到香港，
探索這個精采，忙碌
的都會時，你會遇見
什麼？高聳的摩天
樓？炫亮的金魚？
還是往來於閃閃發
光港灣的渡輪？邊
翻頁邊幻想，因為
"H是香港"！

diǎn
點

xīn
心

Dim Sam

Steamer baskets filled with soft, savory buns
warm a cool morning.

zhēng	lóng	lǐ	kě	kǒu	de	rè
蒸	籠	裡	可	口	的	熱
bāo	zi	wēn	nuǎn	le	hán	lěng
包	子	溫	暖	了	寒	冷
de	zǎo	chén				
的	早	晨				

Star Ferry

From Hong Kong Island to Kowloon,
seven minutes on a floating star

天星小輪

měi	gé	qī	fēn	zhōng	kě	yǐ	chéng
每	隔	七	分	鐘	可	以	乘
shàng	yī	kē	xīng	piāo	liú	wǎng	lái
上	一	顆	星	漂	流	往	來
xiāng	gǎng	dǎo	hé	jiǔ	lóng	zhī	jiān
香	港	島	和	九	龍	之	間

zhōng
中

yaò
藥

Chinese Herbs

A thousand years of tradition wait in a hundred jars of healing herbs.

shàng	qiān	nián	de	chuán	tǒng	zài	shàng
上	千	年	的	傳	統	在	上

bǎi	guàn	yaò	cǎo	zhōng	děng	dài	
百	罐	藥	草	中	等	待	

Incense

Prayers float to heaven on curls of
sandalwood smoke.

dǎo	gào	suí	zhe	niǎo	niǎo	xiāng	yān
禱	告	隨	著	裊	裊	香	煙

fēi	shàng	tiān	táng
飛	上	天	堂

xiāng
huǒ
香火

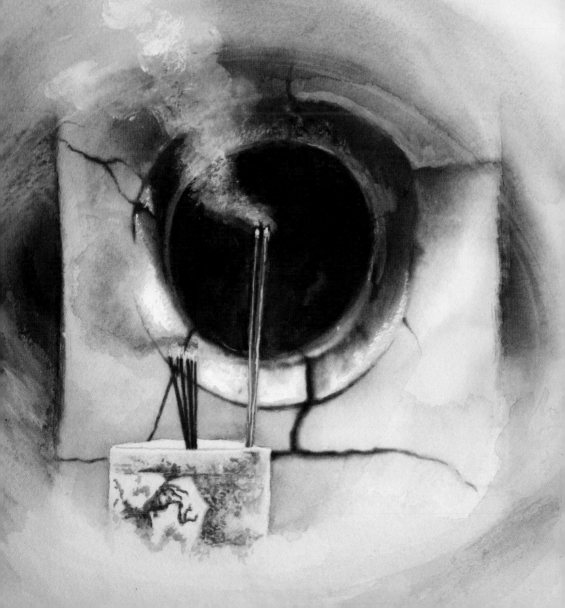

Chess

A circle of men sits captive while red chariot
pursues black general.

suí	zhe	hóng	jū	zhuī	bǔ	hēi	jiāng
隨	著	紅	車	追	捕	黑	將,

zhòng	rén	hóng	fú	lǔ	le		
眾	人	被	俘	擄	了		

Kung Fu

Time, self-discipline and the will to learn
create the art of self-defense.

gōng
功

fū
夫

yòng	shí	jiān	zì	lǜ	hé	jué	xīn
用	時	間，	自	律，	和	決	心

lái	xué	xí	zì	wèi
來	學	習	自	衛

Shoe Repairman

Skillful roadside repair nails a second life to worn out sandals.

lù	biān	de	qiǎo	jiàng	gěi	lèi	huài
路	邊	的	巧	匠	給	累	壞

de	xié	dìng	shàng	dì	èr	chūn	
的	鞋	釘	上	第	二	春	

Abacus

In the expert click of wooden beads
hear shopkeepers measure change.

算 盤

熟 練 的 木 珠 撥 動 聲
中， 聽 得 到 店 家 的 精
打 細 算

shú liàn de mù zhū bō dòng shēng
zhōng ting dé dào diàn jiā de jīng
dǎ xì suàn

suàn pán

Bat

Its wings are quiet, yet a symbol of blessing flies overhead.

biān
蝙
fú
蝠

jí	shǐ	chì	bǎng	jìng	zhǐ	le
即	使	翅	膀	靜	止	了,
cì	fú	hái	shì	gāo	gāo	de
賜	福	還	是	高	高	的
fēi	yáng	zhù				
飛	揚	著				

Goldfish

Carry home a sliver of gold swimming in a silver bubble.

jiāng	yí	piàn	piàn	yōu	yóu	zài
將	一	片	片	悠	游	在
yín	pà	mò	zhōng	de	jīn	bó
銀	泡	沫	中	的	金	箔
dài	huí	jiā				
帶	回	家				

jīn

金

yú

魚

yú
fū
漁夫

Fisherman

Fishermen roam the coastline gathering a harvest of silver fish.

yú	fū	xún	huí	yú	hǎi	àn
漁	夫	巡	迴	於	海	岸
xiàn	yí	lù	shōu	jí	fēng	shèng
線，	一	路	收	集	豐	盛
de	yín	yú				
的	銀	魚				

Parasol

Unfold a pocket of paper shade on a sunny afternoon.

zhǐ 紙
sǎn 傘

yáng guāng càn làn de xià wǔ chēng
陽　光　燦　爛　的　下　午，撐
kāi yī zhǐ dài de yìn liáng
開　一　紙　袋　的　蔭　涼

mó
摩
tiān
天
lóu
樓

Skyscraper

Buildings reach into high clouds like rockets ready to launch.

gāo	lóu	shēn	rù	yún	xiāo	hǎo	xiàng
高	樓	伸	入	雲	霄	好	像

huǒ	jiàn	zhǔn	bèi	fā	shè
火	箭	準	備	發	射

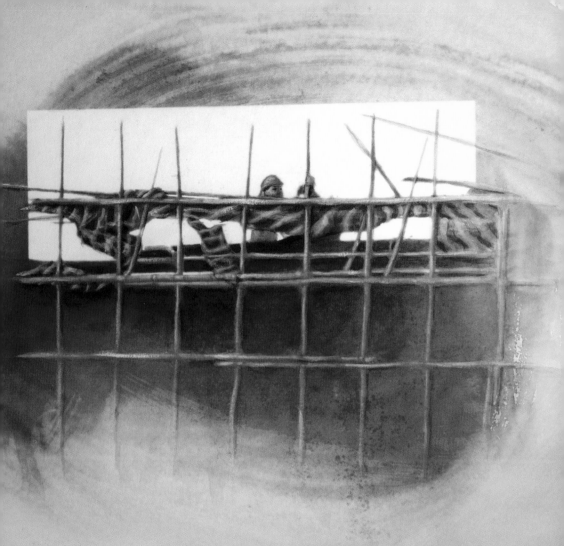

Scaffold

Inside a spiderweb of bamboo cages,
up grows the city.

zhī	zhū	wǎng	shì	de	zhú	jià	lóng
蜘	蛛	網	似	的	竹	架	籠

zhào	xià	dū	shì	chéng	zhǎng	le
罩	下，	都	市	成	長	了

Lion

Lions dance and roar answering the call
of the rumbling drum.

shī	zi	huí	yìng	jí	gǔ	de	zhào
獅	子	回	應	急	鼓	的	召
huàn	ér	hū	xiào	qǐ	wǔ		
喚	而	呼	嘯,	起	舞		

Dragon

Glittering dragon dip and soar, brighten
New Year with your quivering tail.

lóng

龍

guāng	cǎi	duó	mù	de	lóng	shàng	xià
光	彩	奪	目	的	龍	上	下

fēi	wǔ	yǐ	zhàn	dòng	de	wěi	bā
飛	舞,	以	顫	動	的	尾	巴

diǎn	liàng	le	xīn	nián
點	亮	了	新	年

Fan Dancer

Step, twirl, fold and unfold: an early morning dance draws ladies to the park.

wǔ	shàn	zhě

舞
扇
者

kuà	bù	xuán	zhuǎn	hé	shàn	kāi	shàn
跨	步,	旋	轉,	闔	扇,	開	扇,

gōng	yuán	lǐ	de	chén	wǔ	yǐn	lái
公	園	裡	的	晨	舞	引	來

le	chéng	qún	de	shì	nǚ		
了	成	群	的	仕	女		

Cantonese Opera

Love and virtue share the stage with painted
faces and popular songs.

ài	hé	dào	dé	yǔ	xiān	lì	de
愛	和	道	德	與	鮮	麗	的
yóu	cǎi	liǎn	pǔ	jí	liú	xíng	xì
油	彩	臉	譜	及	流	行	戲
qǔ	tóng	tái					
曲	同	台					

guǎng
廣
dōng
東
dà
大
xì
戲

Bird Cage

Songbirds in cages swaying overhead serenade the teahouse with warbling chatter.

niǎo 鳥
lóng 籠

niǎo 鳥	lóng 籠	lǐ 裡	yáo 搖	bǎi 擺	de 的	míng 鳴	què 雀
ràng 讓	chá 茶	guǎn 館	chōng 充	mǎn 滿	yīn 音	yuè 樂	bān 般
de 的	zhōu 啁	jiū 啾	shēng 聲				

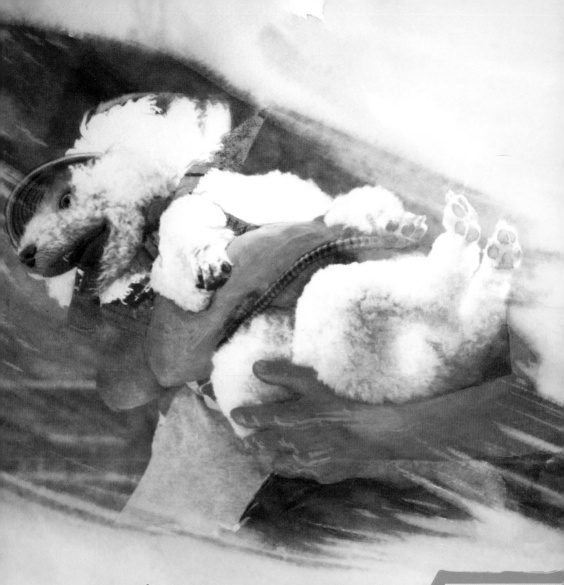

Lapdog

Loving arms hug a petite bundle of panting fur.

小

gǒu

狗

shēn	qíng	de	bì	wān	yōng	bào	zhe
深	情	的	臂	彎	擁	抱	著

yī	xiǎo	tuán	qīng	chuǎn	de	máo	qiú
一	小	團	輕	喘	的	毛	球

Rooster

Paper lanterns glow in the night while a huge autumn moon crowns the sky.

gōng
公
jī
雞

zhǐ	dēng	lóng	zài	jiǎo	jié	de	zhōng
紙	燈	籠	在	皎	潔	的	中

qiū	yuè	yè	lǐ	fā	liàng		
秋	月	夜	裡	發	亮		

Eggballs

Hungry customers wait in line watching
steam rise from sheets of golden waffle.

jī	è	de	gù	kè	pái	duì	děng
飢	餓	的	顧	客	排	隊	等

dài	cóng	zhēng	qì	zhōng	shēng	qǐ	yè
待	從	蒸	氣	中	升	起	頁

yè	jīn	huáng	sè	de	huá	fū	bǐng
頁	金	黃	色	的	華	夫	餅

jī	dàn	zǎi
雞	蛋	仔

Motorbike

City streets rumble with endless waves of shiny motorbikes.

dū	shì	jiē	dào	shàng	shǎn	liàng	de
都	市	街	道	上	閃	亮	的
diàn	dān	chē	cháo	bú	duàn	dì	hōng
電	單	車	潮	不	斷	地	轟
lóng	yáo	gǔn					
隆	搖	滾					

Street Sweeper

Under the brisk swish of a sweeper's broom
boxes and bottles disappear.

清道夫
qīng dào fū

sǎo 掃	zhǒu 帚	qīng 輕	kuài 快	de 的	shā 沙	shā 沙	shā 沙,
hé 盒	zi 子	hé 和	píng 瓶	píng 瓶	guàn 罐	guàn 罐	dōu 都
xiāo 消	shī 失	le 了					

Tai O

dà
大
ào
澳

Drying fish and shrimp paste perfume a village
hidden behind a harbor of stilt houses.

cáng　zài　péng　wū　zhōng　de　yú　cūn,
藏　在　棚　屋　中　的　漁　村，

mí　màn　zhe　xián　yú　hé　xiā　jiàng
瀰　漫　著　鹹　魚　和　蝦　醬

de　fēn　fāng
的　芬　芳

Tram

Riders listen for the "ding-ding!" as double-deckers slide between skyscrapers.

diàn
電
chē
車

zài	dīng	dīng	shēng	lǐ	chéng	kè	dā
在	叮	叮	聲	裡	乘	客	搭

zhe	shuāng	céng	diàn	chē	huá	guò	mó
著	雙	層	電	車	滑	過	摩

tiān	dà	lóu
天	大	樓

Dim Sum Breakfast
Sampan Restaurant, Yung Shue Wan, Lamma
Island

Star Ferry
Seen from Pier #8, Central Business District

Chinese Herbs
Traditional Chinese medicine shop, Aberdeen

Incense Burning
Tin Hau Temple, Lamma Island

Chinese Chess Board
Near Wah Fu Estate & Waterfall, Hong Kong
Island

Kung Fu Master
Sifu Wan Kam Leung, Yau Ma Tei, Kowloon
www.wankamleung.com

Shoe Repairman's Wife Working
Edge of Hollywood Road, Sheung Wan

Abacus
Calculator at Old Couple's Shop on road to Hung
Shing Yeh beach, Yung Shue Wan, Lamma Island

Wooden Bat
Jumbo Restaurant, Aberdeen Marina

Goldfish in Plastic Bags for Sale
Mongkok night market, Kowloon

Fisherman at Work
Lamma Harbor

Parasol Against the Sun
Tsim Sha Tsui, Kowloon

Typical Skyscraper
Aberdeen Square

Bamboo Scaffolding
Queen's Road Central, Hong Kong

Lion Dancer
Wanchai, Convention Center

Dragon
Jumbo Pier, Aberdeen

Fan Dancer
Promenade, Aberdeen Harbor

Cantonese Opera
Chinese New Year, Yung Shue Wan, Lamma Island

Bird Cage
Mongkok bird market, Kowloon

Typical Lapdog
Hung Shing Yeh, Lamma Island

Rooster Lantern Over Chinese New Year
Kowloon Park, Tsim Sha Tsui

Eggballs at Night
Johnston Road, Wanchai

Motorbike
Pizza delivery Vespa, Sheung Wan

Essential Street Sweepers
Yung Shue Wan, Lamma

Tai O
View of Tai O Harbor

Tram
Tram to Sai Ying Pun, Sheung Wan

On This Page
Hong Kong Island: Central, Admiralty & Wanchai
Districts, along Victoria Harbor

Map of Hong Kong

China

Sheung Shui

Tai Po

New Territories

Tai Mo Shan

Tuen Mun

Sha Tin

Chek Lap Kok Internat'l Airport

Kowloon

Mong Kok

Victoria Harbor

TST

Central

Wan Chai

Tai O

Lantau Island

Hong Kong Island

Aberdeen

Lamma Island

South China Sea

Cyanotype: an Antique Blueprint

The cyanotype process begins with a photograph, like this one of a tram weaving through Hong Kong on its way to Sai Ying Pun.

The artist makes a cyanotype print of the photograph by brushing a mixture of special chemicals over paper, placing a negative of her photo on the paper, and exposing it to sunlight. After a few minutes in the light a blue version of the photo appears. This image is called a blueprint.

The artist hand-tints the blueprint to create a softened, many-hued picture.

Tricia Morrissey Ready loves writing children's books because as a child she loved reading them. Born on the edge of one continent (Nairobi, Kenya), she now lives on the edge of another (Vallejo, CA) with her wonderful husband Mark. When she is not reading or writing she enjoys sailing on the San Francisco Bay. The goldfish page is her favorite illustration in this book.

自幼酷愛閱讀童書，因而現在熱衷於編寫兒童圖書．出生在一個洲際邊緣（非洲肯亞奈洛比），目前則與其夫定居另一個洲際邊緣（加州的瓦列霍市）．在閱讀寫作之餘，她極享受揚帆於舊金山灣的樂趣．"金魚"是本書中她最喜愛的一頁．

Elizabeth Briel received her BFA in painting from the University of Minnesota and has since been an itinerant artist, working with the Liverpool Biennial, studying sculpture in Tuscany, and teaching photography to street kids in Cambodia. Her work appears in private collections in Dubai, England, Korea, the USA, Hong Kong, and Norway. She currently lives in Hong Kong but her studio can be anywhere in the world: to make these blueprint photos, she needs only sun and cyan chemicals.

獲得明尼蘇達大學繪畫的藝術學士學位以後，一直是個巡迴藝術家．她曾經參與利物浦雙年展，在托斯卡納學習雕塑，在高棉教導街頭兒童們攝影．目前住在香港，不過她的工作室可以是世界各地．她只需要陽光和青綠色的化學顏料來創造這些藍圖印刷相片．

THINGSASIAN PRESS  *Experience Asia Through the Eyes of Travelers*

"To know the road ahead, ask those coming back."
(CHINESE PROVERB)

East meets West at ThingsAsian Press, where the secrets of Asia are revealed by the travelers who know them best. Writers who have lived and worked in Asia. Writers with stories to tell about basking on the beaches of Thailand, teaching English conversation in the exclusive salons of Tokyo, trekking in Bhutan, haggling with antique vendors in the back alleys of Shanghai, eating spicy noodles on the streets of Jakarta, photographing the children of Nepal, cycling the length of Vietnam's Highway One, traveling through Laos on the mighty Mekong, and falling in love on the island of Kyushu.

Inspired by the many expert, adventurous and independent contributors who helped us build **ThingsAsian.com**, our publications are intended for both active travelers and those who journey vicariously, on the wings of words.

ThingsAsian Press specializes in travel stories, photo journals, cultural anthologies, destination guides and children's books. We are dedicated to assisting readers explore the cultures of Asia through the eyes of experienced travelers.

www.thingsasianpress.com

MORE TITLES FROM THINGSASIAN PRESS:

EVERYDAY LIFE
Through Chinese Peasant Art
By Tricia Morrissey and Ding Sang Mak
6 1/2 x 10 inches; 32 pages;
hardcover; color illustrations
ISBN 978-1-934159-01-9
US $12.95

MY MOM IS A DRAGON
And My Dad Is a Boar
By Tricia Morrissey;
Calligraphy by Kong Lee
6 1/2 x 10 inches; 32 pages;
hardcover; color illustrations
ISBN 978-0-9715940-5-0
US $12.95